Zoe at the Fancy Dress Ball

Written by Susan Reid
Illustrated by Greg Rogers

"What shall I wear
to the fancy dress ball?"
It was all Zoe could think about.

Peter was going as a cowboy.
He had most of his costume already,
even a long lasso.

He felt like a real cowboy.

But the day of the fancy dress ball came and Zoe still didn't know what to wear.

"You'll *have* to decide, Zoe,
or you'll never be ready for the ball,"
said her mother.

Then Zoe had an idea.

"I know!" she said. "I'll be a fairy —
a fairy in a beautiful dress."

"Good!" said her mother. "But there's
no time to make a costume. I'll put
some paper ruffles on your dress."

But Zoe's dress was purple,
and the only paper they could find
was orange.

Zoe moaned.
"A purple and orange fairy!"

None of the fairies in her books
looked like that!

7

"Can I have some pink satin ballet shoes?" Zoe asked.

But her father had already painted her old sandals silver. Zoe was very disappointed.

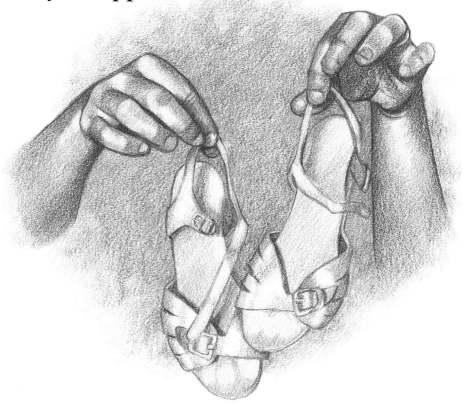

"Cheer up, my girl!" her father teased. "Here's your magic wand. It will give you three wishes."

Zoe didn't think that the painted stick looked like a real magic wand.

She didn't feel like a real fairy, even when she put her wings on.

There was a buzz of excitement
as everyone arrived at the hall.

But while the other children played
and danced, Zoe stayed in her seat.

Then Mrs. Smithers stood up.
"It's time for the judging
of the best costume," she announced.
"Come on, children —
all line up for the grand parade!"

"Oh no!" thought Zoe,
and she gripped her wand tightly.
"I wish no one could see me."

Then a strange thing happened . . .

Suddenly all the lights in the hall
went out. Some people lit candles
that flickered and glowed in the dark.

But no one could make the lights
come on again.

Zoe's father and some other parents
opened the front doors.

They parked their cars right outside,
so that the headlights shone
into the hall.

"Now the grand parade can continue!" said Mrs. Smithers. "It's time to give out the prizes."

Zoe tried to stay out of the light.
"I'll help you, Mrs. Smithers," she said.

After the grand parade there was
one prize left over.
Mrs. Smithers gave it to Zoe.
"This is to thank my little helper,
the good fairy," she said.
"I wish that Zoe could
use her magic wand
to make the lights
come back on."

"I wish the lights
would come on so
that we could have
supper!" said Zoe,
who was feeling
hungry.

Then suddenly the lights came back on.

"Good for you, Zoe!" someone called.
People whistled, clapped, and cheered.
Mrs. Smithers laughed, and shouted
above the noise.

"Our fairy has granted our wish!
Now, supper is served!"

Zoe was beginning to feel like
a real fairy after all.

"Did you really fix the lights?"
some of the children asked Zoe.

Zoe smiled.

"Now I wish for chocolate cake for supper," she said.